FASHION ECLAIR
COLLECTION

ISBN: 979-8-8521-1458-7

FASHION ECLAIR
COLLECTION

Photography
by Dmytro Khoroshaiev

Welcome to the world of haute patisserie! I am delighted to present to you the *Fashion Éclair Collection*, a selection of 13 éclair recipes that will transport you and your taste buds to a realm of flavor and elegance. Within the pages of this recipe book, you will learn how to make pastries that captivate both your palate and your imagination – from fragrant and fruity delights to rich and indulgent creations.

This extraordinary collection includes both innovative recipes as well as beloved classics. With its timeless elegance and beloved flavors, the classic Chocolate Éclair had to feature in this book. Picture delicate choux pastry filled with a silky smooth chocolate custard and adorned with a glossy chocolate glaze. These éclairs are truly a testament to the timeless allure of the classics.

For a zesty twist, savor the tantalizing tang of our Lemon Éclairs. Delicate choux pastry meets a luscious lemon and yuzu curd to create a delightful balance of sweet and citrusy flavors. These éclairs are a breath of fresh air – a burst of sunshine on your summertime dessert table. And for the coffee lovers, allow me to introduce the Tiramisu Éclair. Indulge in the essence of this beloved Italian dessert reimagined. These sweet treats are filled with a luscious coffee-flavored custard and topped with lashings of mascarpone cream to form a sophisticated dessert that will whisk you away to the romantic streets of Italy.

Complete with clear and user-friendly instructions, all recipes in the *Fashion Éclair Collection* are designed to be easy to follow. It doesn't matter whether you're a pastry newbie or a seasoned patissier, you'll find the guidance you need to create these edible works of art. From mastering the choux pastry to achieving the perfect fillings and decorations, we've got you covered every step of the way.

So, prepare to indulge your senses and elevate your dessert repertoire with the *Fashion Éclair Collection*. Join us on this culinary journey and unlock the secrets to éclair perfection.

Tetyana Verbytska

Founder of KICA Academy

| CONTENTS

CLASSIC ÉCLAIR CHOUX PASTE

for 15-20 éclairs 13 cm long

| MAKING THE CHOUX PASTE

Ingredients	Total weight: ~ 760 g	100%
• Water	125 g	16%
• Milk 3.2%	125 g	16%
• Sea salt	4 g	<1%
• Sugar	4 g	<1%
• Inverted sugar	2 g	<1%
• Butter 82%	112 g	15%
• All-purpose flour	138 g	18%
• Whole eggs	250 g	33%

1. Prepare the eggs and butter: process the room temperature eggs with a hand blender until smooth and cut the butter into small pieces.

2. Put salt, sugar and inverted sugar in a saucepan. Inverted sugar prevents the formation of ice crystals in the choux paste and keeps its texture tender and moist for a longer time. If you are not going to freeze the choux paste, you can skip this ingredient.

3. Add the butter, water and milk to the saucepan and heat everything over low heat, stirring occasionally with a whisk.

   TIP
   • *You can make water-based or milk-based choux paste as well. It depends on the result you want to end up with: the milk-based choux paste is a little darker and fattier, while the water-based choux paste is brighter but, at the same time, crunchier.*

4. When the butter has melted completely, increase the heat and bring the mixture to a boil.

5. Remove the mixture from the heat, add the sifted flour and stir thoroughly with the whisk until smooth.

| MAKING THE CHOUX PASTE

6. In order to make sure that all the starch has swelled, place the choux paste back on the stove and heat for two minutes over low heat, stirring actively with a spatula.

7. Transfer the choux paste to a mixer bowl and start mixing it with a paddle attachment, cooling it down to 55-60 °C / 131-140 °F.

8. When the choux paste has reached the required temperature, gradually, in small lots, start to add in the eggs, continuing to mix the choux paste at low speed.

   TIP
   • *The texture of the finished choux paste is checked visually, that's why you might need a little less egg mixture than it is mentioned in the recipe. The choux paste should be smooth, homogeneous, glossy, and fall off the paddle as a ribbon. If you have used all the eggs and the right texture is still not achieved, you can add a little warm milk, but such cases are extremely rare to happen.*

9. Cover the finished choux paste with cling film and leave it to rest at 30 °C / 86 °F for an hour.

Classic Éclair Choux Paste
for 15-20 éclairs 13 cm long

| PIPING THE ÉCLAIRS

Ingredients

- Choux paste
- Cooking oil spray
- Icing sugar   Sufficient quantity

1. Fill a pastry bag fitted with an Open Star tip d=16 mm with the choux paste 2/3 full.

2. Pipe the 12.5-13 cm long éclairs (~35 g each) at a distance 1-1.5 cm over a Teflon-coated baking sheet or a perforated silicone mat. To get perfectly even éclairs, do not move your hands while piping; instead, move your body back.

3. After piping, spray the éclairs with a thin layer of cooking oil, then lightly sprinkle them with icing sugar through a sieve. A thin crust on the surface will protect them from cracking.

4. Put the éclairs in the freezer until they freeze completely. You can store the élairs in the freezer for up to two weeks, just make sure to put them into an airtight container to protect them from drying out.

Classic Éclair Choux Paste
for 15-20 éclairs 13 cm long

| BAKING THE ÉCLAIRS

Ingredients

- Frozen éclairs

1. Preheat the oven to 280 °C / 536 °F and then turn it off.

2. Transfer the frozen éclairs to a perforated silicone mat, keeping a distance of approximately 6 cm between them.

3. Place the éclairs in the turned off oven for 20-25 minutes. During this time, they should rise, acquire the maximum volume and begin to brown slightly. Then turn on the heat at 155-160 °C / 311-320 °F and bake the éclairs for 15-20 minutes more.

4. Finished éclairs should have a uniform golden brown color and a sufficiently hard surface. When pressed, it will crunch slightly, but the inside of the éclair will remain soft and moist. After baking, transfer the éclairs to a wire rack to cool down faster. This can take about 20-30 minutes.

TIP
- *If you want to bake éclairs for future use, let them cool down completely and then freeze them. Baked éclairs can be stored for up to two weeks in the freezer. Then, when you need them, put the frozen éclairs in the oven at 150 °C / 302 °F and bake them for 3-4 minutes.*

BERRY ÉCLAIRS
for 15–20 éclairs 13 cm long

| GELATIN MASS

Ingredients	Total weight: ~ 14 g	100%
• Powdered gelatin 200 Bloom	2 g	14%
• Cold water	12 g	86%

1. Pour the powdered gelatin into a clean container and add cold water. Gently stir with a whisk.

2. Place the mixture in the fridge for 10–15 minutes to allow the gelatin to swell and bloom.

3. Take the mass out of the fridge and melt it in the microwave. If there is any foam, remove it with a sieve. Then place the mass back in the fridge to let it set completely.

4. Use scissors to cut the gelatin mass into cubes — this way, you can weigh it and it's more convenient to work with. The ratio of gelatin to water should always be 1:6 (one part gelatin to six parts water).

5. You can make the gelatin mass in advance and store it in the fridge for up to 2 days.

    TIP
    *   *If you're using gelatin leaves instead, take the same weight as you would with powdered gelatin and soak the leaves in cold water. The gelatin leaves should absorb exactly the right amount of water they need. Then squeeze them and use as required.*

| CLASSIC ÉCLAIR CHOUX PASTE

1. To make the classic choux paste, follow the recipe on page 9.

2. Then pipe the éclairs according to the 'Piping the éclairs' section on page 11.

3. Finally, bake them according to the instructions on page 12.

| VANILLA CHANTILLY CREAM

Ingredients	Total weight: ~ 301 g	100%
• Whipping cream 35% (1)	30 g	10%
• Sugar	20 g	7%
• Gelatin mass	11 g	3%
• Cream cheese	80 g	26%
• Whipping cream 35% (2)	160 g	53%
• Vanilla	½ pod	<1%

1. Pour cream (1) in a saucepan. Add sugar, gelatin mass and vanilla seeds. Warm the mixture up to around 80 °C / 176 °F until the sugar has dissolved and the gelatin mass has melted.

2. Remove the mixture from the heat and add the cream cheese. Mix with a spatula.

3. Pour this mixture in a measuring cup and blend everything with a hand blender to ensure a perfect emulsion. The mixture should turn homogeneous and smooth.

4. Add cold whipping cream (2) to the mixture and mix everything with a spatula. Don't blend the mixture so as not to ruin the fat molecules which are responsible for aeration and stabilization.

5. Cover the Chantilly cream with plastic wrap touching the surface to prevent the skin and condensation from forming. Place it in the fridge for at least 4–6 hours, better overnight.

| VANILLA CHANTILLY CREAM

6. Before using, whip the cream until increased in volume and a light, but stable texture.

| BERRY CREAM

Ingredients	Total weight: ~ 538 g	100%
Cherry puree	111 g	21%
Raspberry puree	111 g	21%
Strawberry puree	111 g	21%
Pectin NH	7 g	1%
Sugar	30 g	6%
Natur Emul Sosa	2 g	<1%
Butter 82%	66 g	12%
Whipping cream 35%	100 g	18%

1. Combine sugar, pectin and Natur Emul using a whisk.

2. Place purees in a saucepan and bring to 35 °C / 95 °F, then gradually add sugar, pectin and Natur Emul mixture, constantly whisking.

3. Bring the mixture to a boil and cook it for 10 seconds, then take the saucepan from the heat, add butter and process with a hand blender until smooth and glossy.

4. Transfer the berry mixture to a clean bowl, cover it with cling film and place in the fridge for 12 hours.

5. After stabilization, stir the mixture well with a whisk until soft and creamy.

6. Pour the cold whipping cream into the bowl of a stand mixer and whip it at medium speed to a semi–whipped texture.

7. Gradually add whipped cream into the berry mixture, constantly mixing with a whisk.

8. Transfer the finished berry cream into a piping bag.

| ASSEMBLING AND DECORATING THE ÉCLAIRS

Ingredients

- Baked éclairs
- Berry cream
- Stabilized vanilla Chantilly cream
- Fresh strawberries 150 g
- Fresh blueberries 50 g
- Fresh raspberries 100 g
- Fresh blackberries 100 g
- Fresh basil leaves 15 g

1. When the éclairs have cooled down, prepare them for filling. To do this, use a needle tip and make three holes in the bottom part of the éclair: two of them close to the edges and one in the middle. These three holes will help you to fill each éclair fully.

2. Fill each hole of the éclair with the berry cream until you feel it is full.

3. Clean off the bottom of the éclair with an offset spatula.

4. Place the stabilized Chantilly cream in the bowl of a stand mixer and whip it at medium speed until light and airy texture, reminiscent of the soft ice cream.

5. Transfer the whipped Chantilly to the piping bag, fitted with a round piping tip   d=10 mm and pipe a strip of the Chantilly on the center of the éclair.

6. Decorate the éclairs with fresh berries and basil leaves by sticking them on the Chantilly cream.

BLACK FOREST ÉCLAIRS

for 15–20 éclairs 13 cm long

Black Forest Éclairs
for 15–20 éclairs 13 cm long

| GELATIN MASS

Ingredients	Total weight: ~ 84 g	100%
• Powdered gelatin 200 Bloom	12 g	14%
• Cold water	72 g	86%

1. Pour the powdered gelatin into a clean container and add cold water. Gently stir with a whisk.

2. Place the mixture in the fridge for 10–15 minutes to allow the gelatin to swell and bloom.

3. Take the mass out of the fridge and melt it in the microwave. If there is any foam, remove it with a sieve. Then place the mass back in the fridge to let it set completely.

4. Use scissors to cut the gelatin mass into cubes — this way, you can weigh it and it's more convenient to work with. The ratio of gelatin to water should always be 1:6 (one part gelatin to six parts water).

5. You can make the gelatin mass in advance and store it in the fridge for up to 2 days.

    TIP
    *   *If you're using gelatin leaves instead, take the same weight as you would with powdered gelatin and soak the leaves in cold water. The gelatin leaves should absorb exactly the right amount of water they need. Then squeeze them and use as required.*

Black Forest Éclairs
for 15–20 éclairs 13 cm long

| CLASSIC ÉCLAIR CHOUX PASTE

1. To make the classic choux paste, follow the recipe on page 9.

2. Then pipe the éclairs according to the 'Piping the éclairs' section on page 11.

3. Finally, bake them according to the instructions on page 12.

| DARK CHOCOLATE NAMELAKA

Ingredients	Total weight: ~ 1017 g	100%
• Milk 3.2%	220 g	22%
• Glucose syrup	11 g	1%
• Gelatin mass	38 g	4%
• Dark chocolate Valrhona Guanaja 70%	309 g	30%
• Whipping cream 35%	439 g	43%

1. Pour the milk and glucose syrup into a saucepan and bring to a boil.

2. Transfer the chocolate and gelatin mass into a measuring cup. Pour the hot milk mixture over it and process with a hand blender until smooth.

3. Cool the emulsion down to 40 °C / 104 °F, add cold whipping cream and mix with a silicone spatula.

4. Cover the namelaka with cling film and place it in the fridge for 6 hours.

| VANILLA WHIPPED GANACHE

Ingredients	Total weight: ~ 1045 g	100%
• White chocolate Valrhona Opalys 33%	180 g	17%
• Whipping cream 35% (1)	410 g	39%
• Whipping cream 35% (2)	410 g	39%
• Xanthan gum	2 g	<1%
• Gelatin mass	43 g	4%
• Vanilla	1 pod	<1%

1. Heat whipping cream (1) and vanilla seeds with the vanilla pod itself to 80 °C / 176 °F. Take the saucepan from the heat, cover with cling film and let the cream infuse for 30 minutes.

2. Combine xanthan gum with melted chocolate using a spatula.

3. Strain the whipping cream and bring it to 80 °C / 176 °F. Pour it onto the chocolate and xanthan gum mixture, add gelatin mass. Process everything with a hand blender until smooth.

4. Cool the emulsion to 40 °C / 104 °F, add cold whipping cream and mix with a spatula.

5. Let the ganache cool down to 3 °C / 37 °F and then place it in the fridge for 6 hours.

Black Forest Éclairs
for 15–20 éclairs 13 cm long

| MACERATED CHERRIES

Ingredients	Total weight: ~ 850 g	100%
• Pitted cherries	400 g	47%
• Sugar	400 g	47%
• Cherry Kirsch liqueur	50 g	6%

1. Pour the sugar into a saucepan, add cherries. Bring the mixture to a boil over medium heat and cook for 20 minutes.

2. Take the saucepan off the heat, let the cherries cool down at room temperature and add cherry Kirsch liqueur.

3. Place the cherries in syrup into the fridge for 12 hours.

4. 30 minutes before assembly, strain the cherries. Put the cherries on a paper towel to remove any excess moisture and syrup.

| CHOCOLATE DÉCOR

Ingredients

- Dark chocolate Valrhona Guanaja 70%   200 g

1. Put a tray in the freezer at least 30 minutes before making the decoration.

2. Temper the chocolate on a marble table. To do this, first, melt the chocolate to 50 °C / 122 °F, then cool it down to 27 °C / 81 °F on the table using a metal scraper. Then again, warm it up to 31 °C / 88 °F with a heat gun. It is ready to be used.

3. Pour the chocolate in a pastry bag and pipe thin lines onto the frozen tray.

4. When the chocolate lines set, cut the sticks of different sizes with a scraper.

Black Forest Éclairs
for 15–20 éclairs 13 cm long

| ASSEMBLING AND DECORATING THE ÉCLAIRS

Ingredients

- Baked éclairs
- Stabilized dark chocolate namelaka
- Stabilized vanilla whipped ganache
- Macerated cherries
- Chocolate décor
- Candied cherries   20 pcs

1. When the éclairs have cooled down, prepare them for filling. To do this, cut a strip 8 cm long and 1 cm wide from the top of each éclair. Keep the removed pieces of baked choux paste.

2. Transfer the vanilla ganache into the bowl of a stand mixer and whip it until light and stable. Transfer the whipped ganache into a piping bag.

3. Fill the éclairs with whipped ganache until almost full. Then place macerated cherries in the center of the éclairs. Pipe a little more ganache on top and smooth it with an offset spatula. Cover it with the stips of choux paste.

4. Transfer the chocolate namelaka into the bowl of a stand mixer and whip it until it acquires a light and pipeable texture. Place the whipped namelaka into a piping bag.

5. Take a third piping bag, fitted with a round tip d=12 mm, and place two pastry bags with whipped namelaka and ganache inside.

6. Pipe a two–colored creamy decoration on top of the éclairs.

7. Garnish the éclairs with chocolate décor and candied cherries.

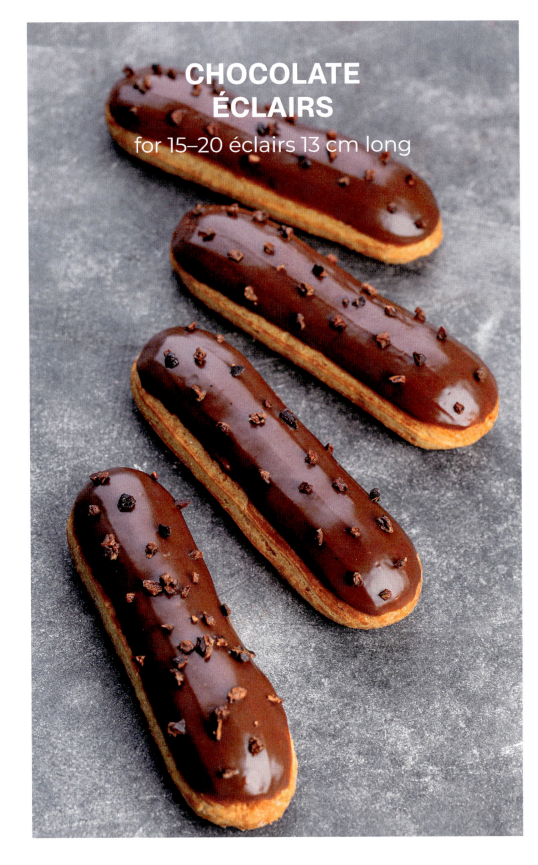

CHOCOLATE ÉCLAIRS
for 15–20 éclairs 13 cm long

Chocolate Éclairs
for 15–20 éclairs 13 cm long

| NEUTRAL GEL (NAPPAGE)

Ingredients	Total weight: ~ 165 g	100%
• Water	72 g	44%
• Sugar (1)	61 g	37%
• Sugar (2)	10 g	6%
• Pectin NH	3.5 g	2%
• Glucose syrup	18 g	11%
• Citric acid powder	0.2 g	<1%

1. Pour the water into a saucepan, add the glucose syrup and sugar (1).

2. Heat the mixture to 30 °C / 86 °F.

3. Mix sugar (2) and pectin NH.

4. Add the pectin and sugar mixture into the saucepan with water, glucose and sugar (1) and bring everything to a boil.

5. Then add citric acid powder. Continue cooking for about 3 minutes.

6. Strain the gel into a clean container and refrigerate.

7. Leave the neutral gel to stabilize in the fridge at 4 °C / 39 °F for at least 6 hours.

Chocolate Éclairs
for 15–20 éclairs 13 cm long

| CHOCOLATE GLAZE

Ingredients	Total weight: ~ 608 g	100%
• Water	73 g	12%
• Condensed milk	75 g	12%
• Sugar	75 g	12%
• Glucose syrup	95 g	16%
• Dark chocolate Callebaut 70%	120 g	20%
• Cocoa butter	20 g	3%
• Neutral gel (nappage)	150 g	25%

1. Pour the water, sugar and glucose syrup into a saucepan and bring to a boil. Cook the syrup up to 104 °C / 219 °F to make it thicker. Take the mixture off the heat and let it cool a little bit.

2. Transfer the dark chocolate, cocoa butter, condensed milk and neutral gel in a measuring cup.

3. Pour in the hot syrup and then process the glaze with a hand blender until a smooth, glossy and stable emulsion has formed.

4. Transfer the glaze into a clean container, cover with cling film touching the surface and let it stabilize in the fridge for at least 6 hours, preferably for 12 hours.

5. Heat the glaze slightly and mix with a hand blender before use.

Chocolate Éclairs
for 15–20 éclairs 13 cm long

| CLASSIC ÉCLAIR CHOUX PASTE

1. To make the classic choux paste, follow the recipe on page 9.

2. Then pipe the éclairs according to the 'Piping the éclairs' section on page 11.

3. Finally, bake them according to the instructions on page 12.

| CHOCOLATE CUSTARD

Ingredients	Total weight: ~ 829 g	100%
• Sugar	44 g	5%
• Cornstarch	30 g	4%
• Egg yolks	30 g	4%
• Whole eggs	40 g	5%
• Milk 3.2%	340 g	41%
• Sea salt	1 g	<1%
• Dark chocolate Callebaut Power 80%	54 g	7%
• Dark chocolate Callebaut 70%	140 g	16%
• Butter 82%	30 g	4%
• Whipping cream 35%	120 g	14%

1. Bring the milk and salt to 80 °C / 176 °F, remove the saucepan from the heat.

2. In a separate bowl, combine sugar and cornstarch, then add the eggs and egg yolks. Stir until combined.

3. Gradually strain the hot milk over the mixture of eggs, sugar and starch.

4. Pour the milk and egg mixture back into the saucepan and cook the custard, heating it over low heat, constantly stirring until it boils. After that, continue cooking it for 1–2 minutes more.

| CHOCOLATE CUSTARD

5. Transfer the chocolate and butter into a measuring cup, pour the hot custard over it and process everything with a hand blender until smooth.

6. Pour the custard in a thin layer in a wide container. Cover it with cling film touching the surface and chill it quickly to 3 °C / 37 °F in a shock freezer. It is important not to freeze the custard.

7. Whip the cold whipping cream with a whisk attachment into a soft foam.

8. Stir the chilled custard with a whisk to get a uniform texture. Add the whipped cream and gently mix with a spatula.

9. Transfer the chocolate custard to the fridge. Like that, it can be stored in a closed container for up to 72 hours.

| HAZELNUT AND ALMOND PRALINE

Ingredients	Total weight: ~ 272 g	100%
• Toasted almonds	95 g	35%
• Toasted hazelnuts	95 g	35%
• Sugar	50 g	18%
• Glucose syrup	30 g	11%
• Sea salt	1.5 g	<1%

1. Toast the nuts in the oven at 130 °C / 266 °F for 40 minutes. Leave them to cool down at room temperature.

2. Pour the glucose syrup into a saucepan, add the sugar. Heat the mixture over medium heat until a very intense caramel color or 185 °C / 365 °F.

3. Pour the finished caramel over the nuts. To highlight the flavor of the nuts, add salt. Optionally, you can add dry vanilla pods left after making other pastries.

4. Leave the nuts to cool down at room temperature until the caramel hardens.

5. Transfer the caramel–coated nuts to a food processor and blend at low speed until you get a paste.

Chocolate Éclairs
for 15–20 éclairs 13 cm long

| CRUNCHY LAYER

Ingredients	Total weight: ~ 150 g	100%
• Milk chocolate Cacao Barry Ghana 40%	20 g	13%
• Hazelnut and almond praline	70 g	47%
• Sea salt	0.5 g	<1%
• Feuilletine (wafer crumbs)	50 g	33%
• Cocoa nibs	10 g	7%

1. Put the praline into a bowl. Add sea salt and milk chocolate, melted to 40 °C / 104 °F.

2. Add wafer crumbs and, for a more pronounced chocolate touch, cocoa nibs. Gently combine all ingredients.

   TIP
   - *Cocoa nibs are an optional ingredient, so you can skip it or replace it with chopped dark chocolate.*

3. Use a 16x16 cm frame and spread the crunchy mixture in it using an offset spatula (you should end up with a layer 0.5 cm thick).

4. When the layer is formed, remove the frame and put the layer into the freezer until it completely sets.

5. The frozen crunchy layer needs to be prepared for assembly. For this, transfer it on a cutting board and cut into strips 8 cm long and 1 cm wide. The size of the strips can be modified depending on the size of your éclairs.

6. Once the strips of a crunchy layer are cut, put them back in the freezer to stabilize and keep like that until assembly.

| ASSEMBLING THE ÉCLAIRS

Ingredients

- Baked éclairs
- Chilled chocolate custard
- Frozen crunchy strips

1. When the éclairs have cooled down, prepare them for filling. To do this, cut a strip 8 cm long and 1 cm wide from the bottom of each éclair. Keep the removed pieces of baked choux paste.

2. Put the chilled custard in the mixer bowl and stir it with a whisk attachment at medium speed until smooth. The same can be made manually with a hand whisk. Use a pastry bag fitted with a round tip d=7 mm and fill 2/3 of it with the custard.

3. Fill the éclairs with custard by guiding the tip from one end to the other, leaving some space for the crunchy layer.

4. Insert the strip of a crunchy layer inside each éclair and press slightly. Use the removed pieces of baked choux paste to seal the bottom.

5. Put the éclairs in the fridge to stabilize for a couple of minutes.

| GLAZING AND DECORATING THE ÉCLAIRS

Ingredients	Total weight: ~ 57 g	100%
• Cocoa beans	25 g	44%
• Sugar	22 g	39%
• Water	10 g	17%
• Chilled assembled éclairs		
• Stabilized chocolate glaze		

1. Combine sugar and water in a saucepan, bring to 117 °C / 243 °F.

2. Pour the sugar syrup over the cocoa beans and let them infuse for 30 minutes.

3. Spread the cocoa beans on a silicone mat and bake at 160 °C / 320 °F for 15 minutes.

4. Cool them down at room temperature.

5. Heat the chocolate glaze to 30 °C / 86 °F and process it with a hand blender.

6. Coat the cooled éclairs by dipping 1/3 of each éclair into the glaze. Carefully remove excess glaze by running your finger over the surface of the éclair.

7. Sprinkle the coated éclairs with cocoa beans.

COCONUT ÉCLAIRS
for 15–20 éclairs 13 cm long

| GELATIN MASS

Ingredients	Total weight: ~ 70 g	100%
• Powdered gelatin 200 Bloom	10 g	14%
• Cold water	60 g	86%

1. Pour the powdered gelatin into a clean container and add cold water. Gently stir with a whisk.

2. Place the mixture in the fridge for 10–15 minutes to allow the gelatin to swell and bloom.

3. Take the mass out of the fridge and melt it in the microwave. If there is any foam, remove it with a sieve. Then place the mass back in the fridge to let it set completely.

4. Use scissors to cut the gelatin mass into cubes — this way, you can weigh it and it's more convenient to work with. The ratio of gelatin to water should always be 1:6 (one part gelatin to six parts water).

5. You can make the gelatin mass in advance and store it in the fridge for up to 2 days.

TIP
• *If you're using gelatin leaves instead, take the same weight as you would with powdered gelatin and soak the leaves in cold water. The gelatin leaves should absorb exactly the right amount of water they need. Then squeeze them and use as required.*

| NEUTRAL GLAZE (NAPPAGE)

Ingredients	Total weight: ~ 180 g	100%
• Water	88 g	44%
• Sugar (1)	74 g	37%
• Sugar (2)	12 g	6%
• Pectin NH	4 g	2%
• Glucose syrup	22 g	11%
• Citric acid powder	0.2 g	<1%

1. Pour the water into a saucepan, add the glucose syrup and sugar (1).

2. Heat the mixture to 30 °C / 86 °F.

3. Mix sugar (2) and pectin NH.

4. Add the pectin and sugar mixture into the saucepan with water, glucose and sugar (1) and bring everything to a boil.

5. Then add citric acid powder. Continue cooking for about 3 minutes.

6. Strain the glaze into a clean container and refrigerate.

7. Leave the neutral glaze to stabilize in the fridge at 4 °C / 39 °F for at least 6 hours.

| MIRROR GLAZE

Ingredients	Total weight: ~ 645 g	100%
• Gelatin mass	70 g	11%
• Whipping cream 35%	90 g	14%
• Water	40 g	6%
• Glucose syrup	65 g	10%
• White chocolate Cacao Barry Zephyr 34%	200 g	31%
• Neutral glaze (nappage)	180 g	28%

1. In a saucepan, combine cream, water and glucose syrup.

2. Bring the mixture to 80 °C / 176 °F and take it off the heat.

3. Add the gelatin mass. Stir with a spatula until it has dissolved completely, then strain.

4. Combine the white chocolate and the neutral glaze in a measuring cup. Strain the hot liquid over the chocolate and neutral glaze.

5. Process the mixture with a hand blender at low speed, trying not to incorporate air bubbles, for 2–3 minutes until smooth.

6. Pour the finished glaze into a clean bowl, cover it with cling film touching the surface so that the glaze does not dry out and the condensation does not form on it, and put it in the fridge for at least 6 hours.

COCONUT GANACHE

Ingredients	Total weight: ~ 929 g	100%
• White chocolate Valrhona Opalys 33%	608 g	65%
• Coconut puree	256 g	27%
• Lemon juice	16 g	2%
• Glucose syrup	24 g	3%
• Inverted sugar	24 g	3%
• Sea salt	1 g	<1%

1. Place coconut puree, lemon juice, glucose syrup and inverted sugar into a saucepan and bring to 80 °C / 176 °F.

2. Transfer white chocolate and salt to a measuring cup, pour the hot puree mixture over it and process with a hand blender until smooth.

3. Pour the ganache into a clean bowl and cover it with cling film.

4. Leave the ganache at room temperature for 3 hours, then transfer in the fridge until it becomes pliable.

CLASSIC ÉCLAIR CHOUX PASTE

1. To make the classic choux paste, follow the recipe on page 9.

2. Then pipe the éclairs according to the 'Piping the éclairs' section on page 11.

3. Finally, bake them according to the instructions on page 12.

Coconut Éclairs
for 15–20 éclairs 13 cm long

| ASSEMBLING THE ÉCLAIRS

Ingredients

- Baked éclairs
- Stabilized coconut ganache

1. When the éclairs have cooled down, prepare them for filling. To do this, use a needle tip and make three holes in the bottom part of the éclair: two of them close to the edges and one in the middle. These three holes will help you to fill each éclair fully.

2. Fill a pastry bag fitted with a round tip d=7 mm with the finished ganache 2/3 full.

3. Fill each hole of the éclair with the ganache until you feel it is full.

4. Clean off the bottom of the éclairs with an offset spatula, transfer the éclairs to a baking sheet and put them in the fridge for 5–10 minutes until the ganache has stabilized.

| COCONUT CURLS

Ingredients

- Fresh coconut   1 pc

1. Crack open the coconut by tapping it around with the back of a knife. Try to tap at the same place each time so it cracks and you get two halves of it.

2. Insert a sharp knife between the flesh and the shell and run it down gently around the coconut to remove the flesh.

3. Rinse the coconut flesh and cut it into thin slices using a vegetable peeler.

| COCONUT CURLS

4. Give the coconut slices a beautiful curved shape by placing them, for example, in a silicone hemisphere mold with cavities d=3 cm.

5. Put the mold with coconut curls in the oven at 40 °C / 104 °F for a few hours until dry. The coconut curls will retain their shape and it will be easy to use them to decorate the éclairs.

| GLAZING AND DECORATING THE ÉCLAIRS

Ingredients

- Chilled assembled éclairs
- Mirror glaze
- Desiccated coconut   200 g
- Coconut curls

1. Heat the glaze to 26 °C / 79 °F and process it with a hand blender until smooth.

2. Coat the cooled éclairs by dipping 1/3 of each éclair into the glaze. Carefully remove excess glaze by running your finger over the surface of the éclair.

3. Sprinkle the glaze coating with desiccated coconut and decorate the éclairs with coconut curls.

CRÈME BRÛLÉE ÉCLAIRS

for 15–20 éclairs 13 cm long

| GELATIN MASS

Ingredients	Total weight: ~ 14 g	100%
• Powdered gelatin 200 Bloom	2 g	14%
• Cold water	12 g	86%

1. Pour the powdered gelatin into a clean container and add cold water. Gently stir with a whisk.

2. Place the mixture in the fridge for 10–15 minutes to allow the gelatin to swell and bloom.

3. Take the mass out of the fridge and melt it in the microwave. If there is any foam, remove it with a sieve. Then place the mass back in the fridge to let it set completely.

4. Use scissors to cut the gelatin mass into cubes — this way, you can weigh it and it's more convenient to work with. The ratio of gelatin to water should always be 1:6 (one part gelatin to six parts water).

5. You can make the gelatin mass in advance and store it in the fridge for up to 2 days.

TIP
- *If you're using gelatin leaves instead, take the same weight as you would with powdered gelatin and soak the leaves in cold water. The gelatin leaves should absorb exactly the right amount of water they need. Then squeeze them and use as required.*

| NEUTRAL GLAZE (NAPPAGE)

Ingredients	Total weight: ~ 165 g	100%
• Water	72 g	44%
• Sugar (1)	61 g	37%
• Sugar (2)	10 g	6%
• Pectin NH	3.5 g	2%
• Glucose syrup	18 g	11%
• Citric acid powder	0.2 g	<1%

1. Pour the water into a saucepan, add the glucose syrup and sugar (1).

2. Heat the mixture to 30 °C / 86 °F.

3. Mix sugar (2) and pectin NH.

4. Add the pectin and sugar mixture into the saucepan with water, glucose and sugar (1) and bring everything to a boil.

5. Then add citric acid powder. Continue cooking for about 3 minutes.

6. Strain the glaze into a clean container and refrigerate.

7. Leave the neutral glaze to stabilize in the fridge at 4 °C / 39 °F for at least 6 hours.

| CLASSIC ÉCLAIR CHOUX PASTE

1. To make the classic choux paste, follow the recipe on page 9.

2. Then pipe the éclairs according to the 'Piping the éclairs' section on page 11.

3. Finally, bake them according to the instructions on page 12.

| CARAMEL CUSTARD

Ingredients	Total weight: ~ 888 g	100%
Milk 3.2%	400 g	45%
Whipping cream 35%	100 g	11%
Egg yolks	80 g	9%
Sugar	94 g	10%
Cornstarch	40 g	4%
Butter 82%	110 g	12%
Gelatin mass	14 g	2%
Greek yogurt	50 g	6%

1. Place sugar in a saucepan and bring to 180 °C / 356 °F over medium heat.

2. Pour the caramel on a silicone mat or parchment paper and leave it to cool down at room temperature.

3. Place the chilled caramel in a food processor and grind it into fine powder.

4. In a separate bowl, combine powdered caramel and cornstarch, add the egg yolks. Stir until a light, homogeneous mass is obtained.

5. In a saucepan, heat the milk and cream to 80 °C / 176 °F. Gradually strain the hot milk over the mixture of yolks, sugar and starch.

| CARAMEL CUSTARD

6. Pour the milk and cream mixture back into the saucepan and cook the custard on low heat, constantly stirring, until it boils. After that, boil it for 1–2 minutes more.

7. Add the gelatin mass to the custard and stir until it has dissolved. Cool the custard down to 40 °C / 104 °F by placing it over a cold water bath, or leave it at room temperature, stirring occasionally to avoid skin forming.

8. Once the custard has cooled down, gradually add in the room temperature butter (18–20 °C / 64–68 °F) and stir the custard with a whisk.

9. Add greek yogurt and stir with a whisk once again.

10. Transfer the finished custard to a clean and wide container and let it cool down quickly. Cover it with cling film touching the surface and put it in the fridge or freezer for 10–15 minutes.

11. After cooling, the custard is ready to be used. It can be stored in the fridge for 48 h.

| ASSEMBLING THE ÉCLAIRS

Ingredients

- Baked éclairs
- Chilled caramel custard

1. When the éclairs have cooled down, prepare them for filling. To do this, use a needle tip and make three holes in the bottom part of the éclair: two of them close to the edges and one in the middle. These three holes will help you to fill each éclair fully.

2. Place the custard in a mixer bowl and stir with a whisk attachment at high speed until smooth. This can also be done by hand.

3. Fill a pastry bag fitted with a round tip d=7 mm with the custard 2/3 full.

4. Fill each hole of the éclair with the custard until you feel it is full.

5. Clean off the bottom of the éclairs with an offset spatula, transfer the éclairs to a baking sheet and put them in the fridge for 5–10 minutes until the custard has stabilized.

| DECORATING THE ÉCLAIRS

Ingredients

- Chilled assembled éclairs
- Sugar paste (rolled fondant)   200 g
- Brown sugar   150 g
- Water   50 g
- Cornstarch   25 g
- Neutral glaze (nappage)   100 g

1. Knead the sugar paste in your hands until soft and plastic.

2. Sprinkle the work surface with cornstarch, and roll out the pasta to a thickness of 2 mm.

3. Using an éclair cutter, cut out 20 strips of sugar paste.

4. Heat the neutral glaze to 80 °C / 176 °F and brush the top of the éclairs with it, place the sugar paste on top and press lightly to stick it well.

5. Brush each sugar paste strip with water using a pastry brush. Sprinkle it with some brown sugar and caramelize it using a blow torch.

HAZELNUT ÉCLAIRS
for 15–20 éclairs 13 cm long

| CLASSIC ÉCLAIR CHOUX PASTE

1. To make the classic choux paste, follow the recipe on page 9.

2. Then pipe the éclairs according to the 'Piping the éclairs' section on page 11.

3. Finally, bake them according to the instructions on page 12.

| HAZELNUT PRALINE

Ingredients	Total weight: ~ 670 g	100%
• Hazelnuts with skin	400 g	60%
• Sugar	266 g	39%
• Sea salt	4 g	<1%

1. Roast the hazelnuts at 130 °C / 266 °F for 30 minutes. Let them cool down at room temperature. Do not remove the skin.

2. Cook the sugar in a saucepan to an amber color or to 180–185 °C / 356–365 °F.

3. Pour the caramel onto a silicone mat and sprinkle the hazelnuts and sea salt on top. Let the caramel cool down at room temperature.

4. Then put everything in a food processor and blend until you get a semi liquid texture. When the praline is ready, store it at room temperature in a closed container.

| CUSTARD

Ingredients	Total weight: ~ 565 g	100%
• Milk 3.2%	375 g	66%
• Egg yolks	80 g	14%
• Sugar	70 g	12%
• All–purpose flour	20 g	4%
• Cornstarch	20 g	4%

1. Pour the milk into a saucepan and heat it up.

2. Whisk the egg yolks and sugar in a separate bowl until they lighten in color.

3. Incorporate flour and cornstarch into the egg mixture.

4. Pour some milk into the mixture, stirring constantly.

5. Transfer the mixture back into the saucepan and bring it to a boil while whisking. Let it cook for around 2–3 minutes.

6. Immediately pour the custard in a baking tray lined with a guitar sheet to cool it down faster.

7. Cling–wrap the custard and leave it in the fridge until it cools down completely.

| MERINGUE

Ingredients	Total weight: ~ 141 g	100%
• Glucose syrup	88 g	62%
• Egg whites	53 g	38%

1. Pour the glucose syrup into a bowl.

| MERINGUE

2. Add the egg whites and warm the mixture slightly over a water bath to 40 °C / 104 °F.

3. Pour the mixture into a mixing bowl and whip it using a whisk attachment into a stable meringue.

| HAZELNUT BUTTERCREAM

Ingredients	Total weight: ~ 1110 g	100%
• Butter 82%	240 g	22%
• Hazelnut praline	240 g	22%
• Custard	500 g	45%
• Meringue	130 g	11%

1. Stir the cold custard in a planetary mixer with a paddle attachment and put it back in the fridge.

2. Whip the soft butter with the praline until light and airy.

3. Gently incorporate the chilled custard.

4. Mix well, carefully folding the meringue in.

| CHOCOLATE DÉCOR

Ingredients	
• White chocolate 33%	200 g
• Chopped hazelnuts	100 g

1. Wipe the back of a baking tray with a damp sponge, apply a guitar sheet to it and smooth it with a scraper.

| CHOCOLATE DÉCOR

2. Spread the tempered chocolate in a thin layer over the guitar sheet, and sprinkle with chopped hazelnuts.

3. Cut chocolate strips with an éclair cutter.

4. Cover the chocolate with a sheet of parchment paper and another baking tray.

5. Leave the chocolate to crystallize at room temperature for 12 hours.

| ASSEMBLING AND DECORATING THE ÉCLAIRS

Ingredients

- Baked éclairs
- Hazelnut buttercream
- Leftover hazelnut praline
- Chocolate décor
- Hazelnut skins   Sufficient quantity

1. When the éclairs have cooled down, prepare them for filling. To do this, cut a strip 8 cm long and 1 cm wide from the top of each éclair.

2. Transfer the hazelnut buttercream into the piping bag, fitted with a Closed Star tip d=7 mm and fill 2/3 of the éclairs with it.

3. Transfer the praline into the piping bag and pipe it into the center of each éclair.

4. Pipe a little more buttercream on the top and smooth it with an offset spatula. Then pipe a creamy decoration on the top.

5. Place chocolate décor on the buttercream and decorate the finished éclairs with hazelnut skins.

HONEY CAKE ÉCLAIRS

for 15–20 éclairs 13 cm long

| GELATIN MASS

Ingredients	Total weight: ~ 42 g	100%
• Powdered gelatin 200 Bloom	6 g	14%
• Cold water	36 g	86%

1. Pour the powdered gelatin into a clean container and add cold water. Gently stir with a whisk.

2. Place the mixture in the fridge for 10–15 minutes to allow the gelatin to swell and bloom.

3. Take the mass out of the fridge and melt it in the microwave. If there is any foam, remove it with a sieve. Then place the mass back in the fridge to let it set completely.

4. Use scissors to cut the gelatin mass into cubes — this way, you can weigh it and it's more convenient to work with. The ratio of gelatin to water should always be 1:6 (one part gelatin to six parts water).

5. You can make the gelatin mass in advance and store it in the fridge for up to 2 days.

TIP

• *If you're using gelatin leaves instead, take the same weight as you would with powdered gelatin and soak the leaves in cold water. The gelatin leaves should absorb exactly the right amount of water they need. Then squeeze them and use as required.*

| CLASSIC ÉCLAIR CHOUX PASTE

1. To make the classic choux paste, follow the recipe on page 9.

2. Then pipe the éclairs according to the 'Piping the éclairs' section on page 11.

3. Finally, bake them according to the instructions on page 12.

| SOUR CREAM CHANTILLY

Ingredients	Total weight: ~ 896 g	100%
• Whipping cream 35% (1)	50 g	6%
• Sugar	50 g	6%
• Gelatin mass	40 g	4%
• Sour cream 30%	236 g	26%
• Whipping cream 35% (2)	520 g	58%

1. Pour the cream (1) into a saucepan, add gelatin mass and sugar. Heat the cream to 80 °C / 176 °F to make the sugar and gelatin dissolve.

2. Transfer the sour cream into a measuring cup and gradually pour in the hot cream, sugar and gelatin mixture. Process the mixture with a hand blender.

   TIP
   • *In this recipe you can substitute sour cream for cream cheese.*

3. Pour cold cream (2) into the mixture and stir thoroughly with a spatula.

4. Cover the Chantilly cream with cling film touching the surface and put it in the fridge for 12 hours to stabilize.

| HONEY SPONGE

Ingredients for 1 baking frame 16x16 cm	Total weight: ~ 260 g	100%
• Whole eggs	62 g	24%
• Buckwheat honey	32 g	12%
• All–purpose flour	32 g	13%
• Buckwheat flour	30 g	11%
• Icing sugar	30 g	11%
• Sea salt	1 g	<1%
• Baking powder	2.5 g	1%
• Milk 2.5%	20 g	8%
• Butter 82%	50 g	19%

1. Mix sifted all–purpose flour, buckwheat flour, icing sugar, baking powder and sea salt with a whisk. Set the mixture aside.

2. In a separate bowl, combine room temperature whole eggs and honey using a whisk.

3. Add the egg mixture to the dry ingredients and mix with a whisk until combined.

4. Add the room temperature milk and butter, melted to 50–55 °C / 122–131 °F. Mix well with a whisk.

5. Prepare a baking tray with a piece of parchment paper and a baking frame 16x16 cm. Spread the batter in the frame in an even layer using an offset spatula.

6. Bake the sponge at 170 °C / 338 °F for 10–12 minutes. The properly baked sponge should be golden brown and spring back when pressed lightly.

7. Let the baked honey sponge cool down at room temperature for about 30 minutes.

| HONEY SPONGE

8. When the sponge is completely cooled, carefully cut it out of the frame. Cut the sponge into 10 strips measuring 1x7 cm and leave them at room temperature, cling–wrapped, until assembly.

9. Place the leftover sponge in the food–processor and grind it until fine crumbs are obtained. Sift through a large sieve.

10. Dry the crumbs in the oven at 100 °C / 212 °F for about 1 hour.

| HONEY SYRUP

Ingredients	Total weight: ~ 200 g	100%
• Water	180 g	90%
• Honey	20 g	10%

1. Bring water to a boil, take it from the heat and add honey. Mix until the honey has completely dissolved.

2. Allow the syrup to cool down to room temperature.

| SUGAR FLOWERS

Ingredients

• Sugar paste (rolled fondant)	100 g
• Cornstarch	20 g
• White chocolate 30%	50 g
• Yellow fat–soluble colorant	1 g

1. Knead the sugar paste in your hands until soft and plastic.

2. Sprinkle the work surface with cornstarch, and roll out the sugar paste to a thickness of 1 mm.

3. Using a flower–shaped cutter d=1 cm cut out the sugar flowers and give them a concave shape.

4. Mix chocolate with yellow colorant and pipe a drop of the chocolate on the center of each flower.

ASSEMBLING AND DECORATING THE ÉCLAIRS

Ingredients

- Baked éclairs
- Baked honey sponge strips
- Honey syrup
- Stabilized sour cream Chantilly
- Honey sponge crumbs
- Sugar flowers

1. When the éclairs have cooled down, prepare them for filling. To do this, cut a strip 8 cm long and 1 cm wide from the top of each éclair.

2. Transfer the sour cream Chantilly into the mixing bowl and whip it into medium–soft peaks using a whisk attachment. Start to whip the cream at medium speed, gradually increasing it to the maximum.

3. Fill the éclairs with the cream by guiding the tip from one end to the other, leaving some space for the honey sponge.

4. Dip the sponge strips in the honey syrup and place them inside each éclair. Press slightly.

5. Pipe a thin line of the Chantilly cream on top of the sponge and smooth it with an offset spatula.

6. Transfer the leftover cream into the piping bag, fitted with a round tip d=12 mm and pipe a creamy decoration on the top.

7. Dust the creamy domes with honey sponge crumbs and decorate with sugar flowers.

LEMON ÉCLAIRS

for 15–20 éclairs 13 cm long

| GELATIN MASS

Ingredients	Total weight: ~ 21 g	100%
• Powdered gelatin 200 Bloom	3 g	14%
• Cold water	18 g	86%

1. Pour the powdered gelatin into a clean container and add cold water. Gently stir with a whisk.

2. Place the mixture in the fridge for 10–15 minutes to allow the gelatin to swell and bloom.

3. Take the mass out of the fridge and melt it in the microwave. If there is any foam, remove it with a sieve. Then place the mass back in the fridge to let it set completely.

4. Use scissors to cut the gelatin mass into cubes — this way, you can weigh it and it's more convenient to work with. The ratio of gelatin to water should always be 1:6 (one part gelatin to six parts water).

5. You can make the gelatin mass in advance and store it in the fridge for up to 2 days.

TIP
• *If you're using gelatin leaves instead, take the same weight as you would with powdered gelatin and soak the leaves in cold water. The gelatin leaves should absorb exactly the right amount of water they need. Then squeeze them and use as required.*

CLASSIC ÉCLAIR CHOUX PASTE

1. To make the classic choux paste, follow the recipe on page 9.

2. Then pipe the éclairs according to the 'Piping the éclairs' section on page 11.

3. Finally, bake them according to the instructions on page 12.

LEMON AND YUZU CURD

Ingredients	Total weight: ~ 876 g	100%
• Lemon juice	100 g	11%
• Yuzu puree	25 g	3%
• Sugar	125 g	14%
• Whole eggs	193 g	22%
• Egg yolks	155 g	18%
• Butter 82%	250 g	29%
• Gelatin mass	21 g	2%
• Lemon zest	7 g	1%

1. Mix sugar with lemon zest using a whisk.

2. Add whole eggs and egg yolks and mix with a whisk until homogeneous.

3. In a saucepan, heat the lemon juice and yuzu puree to 80 °C / 176 °F. Pour the hot mixture over the egg mixture and mix well with a whisk.

4. Pour the lemon and egg mixture back into the saucepan and cook the curd over low heat, constantly stirring, until 82–84 °C / 179–183 °F.

5. Take the saucepan from the heat and strain. Add the gelatin mass and stir until it has dissolved completely.

| LEMON AND YUZU CURD

6. Cool the curd down to 40 °C / 104 °F over a cold water bath, or leave it at room temperature, stirring occasionally to avoid skin forming.

7. Once the curd has cooled down, gradually add butter (16 °C / 60 °F) and stir the curd with a whisk.

8. Transfer the finished curd to a clean and wide container and cool it down quickly. Cover it with cling film touching the surface and put it in the fridge or freezer for 10–15 minutes.

9. After cooling, the curd is ready to be used. It can be stored in the fridge for 72 hours.

| LEMON GEL

Ingredients	Total weight: ~ 188 g	100%
• Water	40 g	21%
• Lemon juice	115 g	61%
• Sugar	30 g	16%
• Agar–agar	3 g	2%

1. Pour water into a saucepan, and while the water is not yet heated, add a mixture of sugar and agar–agar. Turn on a high heat and add lemon juice.

2. Bring the mixture to a boil and simmer it for 30 seconds, stirring occasionally to activate the agar–agar.

3. Remove the saucepan from the stove and pour the gel into a wide container to cool it down quicker. Transfer the gel to the fridge until it sets completely.

ASSEMBLING THE ÉCLAIRS

Ingredients

• Baked éclairs
• Chilled lemon and yuzu curd

1. When the éclairs have cooled down, prepare them for filling. To do this, use a needle tip and make three holes in the bottom part of the éclair: two of them close to the edges and one in the middle. These three holes will help you to fill each éclair fully.

2. Mix the curd in a mixer with a whisk attachment at high speed or by hand until smooth. Fill a pastry bag fitted with a round tip d=7 mm with the finished curd 2/3 full.

3. Fill each hole of the éclair with the curd until you feel it is full.

4. Clean off the bottom of the éclairs with an offset spatula, transfer the éclairs to a baking sheet and put them in the fridge for 5–10 minutes until the curd stabilizes.

| SWISS MERINGUE

Ingredients	Total weight: ~ 150 g	100%
• Egg whites	50 g	33%
• Sugar	100 g	67%

1. Combine the egg whites and sugar in a bowl and place it over a saucepan with boiling water. Cook the mixture, whisking constantly, until it reaches 60 °C / 140 °F.

2. Remove the mixture from the heat and transfer it into a bowl of a stand mixer. Whip it on medium speed until a stable and glossy meringue has formed.

3. Use it immediately.

| DECORATING THE ÉCLAIRS

Ingredients

- Chilled assembled éclairs
- Swiss meringue
- Stabilized lemon gel
- Lemon zest   10 g

1. Transfer the Swiss meringue in the piping bag, fitted with a Closed Star piping tip d=12 mm.

2. Pipe the meringue on top of the éclairs and use a blowtorch to slightly brown it.

3. Transfer the lemon gel to a measuring cup and process it with a hand blender at low speed until a glossy and smooth texture is obtained.

4. Fill a paper cornet with it and pipe drops of gel on the meringue.

5. Decorate the éclairs with fresh lemon zest.

MANGO AND PASSION FRUIT ÉCLAIRS

for 15–20 éclairs 13 cm long

| GELATIN MASS

Ingredients	Total weight: ~ 70 g	100%
• Powdered gelatin 200 Bloom	10 g	14%
• Cold water	60 g	86%

1. Pour the powdered gelatin into a clean container and add cold water. Gently stir with a whisk.

2. Place the mixture in the fridge for 10–15 minutes to allow the gelatin to swell and bloom.

3. Take the mass out of the fridge and melt it in the microwave. If there is any foam, remove it with a sieve. Then place the mass back in the fridge to let it set completely.

4. Use scissors to cut the gelatin mass into cubes — this way, you can weigh it and it's more convenient to work with. The ratio of gelatin to water should always be 1:6 (one part gelatin to six parts water).

5. You can make the gelatin mass in advance and store it in the fridge for up to 2 days.

TIP
  • *If you're using gelatin leaves instead, take the same weight as you would with powdered gelatin and soak the leaves in cold water. The gelatin leaves should absorb exactly the right amount of water they need. Then squeeze them and use as required.*

| NEUTRAL GLAZE (NAPPAGE)

Ingredients	Total weight: ~ 180 g	100%
• Water	88 g	44%
• Sugar (1)	74 g	37%
• Sugar (2)	12 g	6%
• Pectin NH	4 g	2%
• Glucose syrup	22 g	11%
• Citric acid powder	0.2 g	<1%

1. Pour the water into a saucepan, add the glucose syrup and sugar (1).

2. Heat the mixture to 30 °C / 86 °F.

3. Mix sugar (2) and pectin NH.

4. Add the pectin and sugar mixture into the saucepan with water, glucose and sugar (1) and bring everything to a boil.

5. Then add citric acid powder. Continue cooking for about 3 minutes.

6. Strain the glaze into a clean container and refrigerate.

7. Leave the neutral glaze to stabilize in the fridge at 4 °C / 39 °F for at least 6 hours.

| MIRROR GLAZE

Ingredients	Total weight: ~ 647 g	100%
• Gelatin mass	70 g	11%
• Whipping cream 35%	90 g	14%
• Water	40 g	6%
• Glucose syrup	65 g	10%
• White chocolate Cacao Barry Zephyr 34%	200 g	31%
• Neutral glaze (nappage)	180 g	28%
• Yellow water–soluble colorant	2 g	<1%

1. In a saucepan, combine cream, water and glucose syrup.

2. Heat the mixture over low heat to 80 °C / 176 °F and remove from the stove.

3. Add the gelatin mass and stir with a spatula until it has dissolved completely.

4. Combine white chocolate and neutral glaze in a measuring cup. Add the colorant. Strain the hot mixture over the chocolate and neutral glaze.

5. Process everything with a hand blender at low speed, trying not to incorporate air bubbles, for 2–3 minutes so that the colorant has completely dissolved and the glaze has become evenly colored.

6. Pour the finished glaze into a clean bowl, cover it with cling film touching the surface and put it in the fridge for at least 6 hours.

| MANGO CREAM

Ingredients	Total weight: ~ 630 g	100%
• Mango puree	500 g	80%
• Pectin NH	10 g	2%
• Sugar	30 g	5%
• Natur Emul Sosa	6 g	<1%
• Butter 82%	84 g	13%

1. Put the saucepan with mango puree over low heat and bring it to 30–35 °C / 86–95 °F.

2. In a separate bowl, mix the pectin NH, Natur Emul and sugar.

   TIP
   - *With no risk of changing the texture, Natur Emul can be safely replaced by soy or sunflower powdered lecithin.*

3. Once the puree has heated, gradually sprinkle in the mixture of pectin, emulsifier and sugar. Keep mixing everything with a whisk and let the mixture boil for 30 seconds.

4. Remove the saucepan from the heat and transfer the puree to a high measuring cup.

5. Add the butter cut into cubes and process with a hand blender.

   TIP
   - *This recipe calls for sweet cream butter, but if desired, you can replace it with coconut or cocoa butter.*

| MANGO CREAM

6. To help the mango cream cool down quicker, transfer it to a wide flat container and cover it with cling film touching the surface. Put the container in the freezer until completely cooled down (for 15–20 minutes approximately). Once the cream has cooled, place it in the fridge. When leaving the cream in the freezer, be extremely careful to not let it freeze. Otherwise, the structure of the cream will be destroyed.

7. To make the texture of the cream smoother, gently mix it in the mixer with a whisk attachment. The same procedure can be done by hand.

8. Use a pastry bag fitted with a 7 mm round tip and fill it with the finished mango cream 2/3 full.

| MANGO AND PASSION FRUIT CONFIT

Ingredients	Total weight: ~ 193 g	100%
• Mango puree	100 g	52%
• Passion fruit puree (with seeds)	60 g	31%
• Glucose syrup	15 g	8%
• Sugar	15 g	8%
• Pectin NH	2.8 g	1%

1. Pour mango and passion fruit puree in a saucepan.

TIP

• *For this recipe, you can either purchase the frozen / pasteurized puree or use the homemade one.*

2. Add glucose syrup and bring the mixture to 30–35 °C / 86–95 °F.

| MANGO AND PASSION FRUIT CONFIT

3. In the meantime, in a separate bowl mix the sugar with the pectin NH. Once the puree has heated, gradually incorporate the sugar and pectin mixture, stirring constantly with a whisk.

4. Increase the heat and bring the puree to a boil while continuing to mix it with a whisk. Cook it for 30 seconds more and remove from the heat.

5. Transfer the confit to a clean container, cover it with cling film touching the surface and let it cool down completely in the fridge.

6. Use your silicone spatula or whisk to soften the texture of the confit before use. Take the piping bag without a tip and fill it with the confit. Trim the end of the piping bag to fit the passion fruit seed.

| CLASSIC ÉCLAIR CHOUX PASTE

1. To make the classic choux paste, follow the recipe on page 9.

2. Then pipe the éclairs according to the 'Piping the éclairs' section on page 11.

3. Finally, bake them according to the instructions on page 12.

| ASSEMBLING THE ÉCLAIRS

Ingredients

- Baked éclairs
- Chilled mango cream
- Chilled mango and passion fruit confit

1. When the éclairs have cooled down, prepare them for filling. To do this, use a needle tip and make three holes in the bottom part of the éclair: two of them close to the edges and one in the middle. These three holes will help you to fill each éclair fully.

2. Fill each hole of the éclair with the mango cream until you feel it is full.

3. Then, fill each hole of the éclair with the mango and passion fruit confit.

4. Clean off the bottom of the éclairs with an offset spatula and transfer them to a baking sheet and put them in the fridge for 5–10 minutes until the filling stabilizes.

| GLAZING THE ÉCLAIRS

Ingredients

- Chilled assembled éclairs
- Mirror glaze
- Green water–soluble colorant   2 g
- Red water–soluble colorant   2 g
- Orange water–soluble colorant   2 g
- Black water–soluble colorant   2 g
- Water   800 g
- Snow sugar   100 g

1. Heat the mirror glaze to 26 °C / 79 °F and process it with a hand blender until smooth.

2. Coat the cooled éclairs with white icing by dipping each éclair by 1/3 into the glaze. Carefully remove excess glaze by running your finger over the surface of the éclair.

3. Use four different vessels to mix each food colorant with 200 g of water.

4. Pour the green–colored spraying mixture into an airbrush and apply it to the surface of the éclair. Do the same with other mixtures.

5. Sprinkle the colored éclairs with snow sugar.

MATCHA ÉCLAIRS

for 15–20 éclairs 13 cm long

| GELATIN MASS

Ingredients	Total weight: ~ 84 g	100%
• Powdered gelatin 200 Bloom	12 g	14%
• Cold water	72 g	86%

1. Pour the powdered gelatin into a clean container and add cold water. Gently stir with a whisk.

2. Place the mixture in the fridge for 10–15 minutes to allow the gelatin to swell and bloom.

3. Take the mass out of the fridge and melt it in the microwave. If there is any foam, remove it with a sieve. Then place the mass back in the fridge to let it set completely.

4. Use scissors to cut the gelatin mass into cubes — this way, you can weigh it and it's more convenient to work with. The ratio of gelatin to water should always be 1:6 (one part gelatin to six parts water).

5. You can make the gelatin mass in advance and store it in the fridge for up to 2 days.

TIP

• *If you're using gelatin leaves instead, take the same weight as you would with powdered gelatin and soak the leaves in cold water. The gelatin leaves should absorb exactly the right amount of water they need. Then squeeze them and use as required.*

| NEUTRAL GLAZE (NAPPAGE)

Ingredients	Total weight: ~ 180 g	100%
• Water	88 g	44%
• Sugar (1)	74 g	37%
• Sugar (2)	12 g	6%
• Pectin NH	4 g	2%
• Glucose syrup	22 g	11%
• Citric acid powder	0.2 g	<1%

1. Pour the water into a saucepan, add the glucose syrup and sugar (1).

2. Heat the mixture to 30 °C / 86 °F.

3. Mix sugar (2) and pectin NH.

4. Add the pectin and sugar mixture into the saucepan with water, glucose and sugar (1) and bring everything to a boil.

5. Then add citric acid powder. Continue cooking for about 3 minutes.

6. Strain the glaze into a clean container and refrigerate.

7. Leave the neutral glaze to stabilize in the fridge at 4 °C / 39 °F for at least 6 hours.

| GLUTEN–FREE CHOUX PASTE

Ingredients	Total weight: ~ 766 g	100%
• Milk 3.2%	250 g	33%
• Sea salt	4 g	<1%
• Inverted sugar	2 g	<1%
• Butter 82%	110 g	14%
• Rice flour	150 g	20%
• Whole eggs	250 g	33%

1. Prepare the eggs and the butter: process the room temperature eggs with a hand blender until smooth and cut the butter into small pieces.

2. Put salt and inverted sugar in a saucepan. Inverted sugar prevents the formation of ice crystals in the choux paste and keeps its texture tender and moist for a longer time. If you are not going to freeze the choux paste, you can skip this ingredient.

3. Add the butter and milk to the saucepan and heat over low heat, stirring occasionally with a whisk.

   TIP
   • *You can make water–based or milk–based choux paste as well. It depends on the result you want to end up with: the milk–based choux paste is a little darker and fattier, while the water–based choux paste is brighter but, at the same time, crunchier.*

4. When the butter has melted completely, increase the heat and bring the mixture to a strong boil.

5. Remove the mixture from the heat, add the sifted rice flour and stir thoroughly with a whisk until smooth. At this stage, the paste should have a slightly crumbly texture.

| GLUTEN–FREE CHOUX PASTE

6. To make sure that all the starch has swelled, place the choux paste back on the stove and cook it for two minutes over low heat, stirring actively with a silicone spatula.

7. Transfer the choux paste to the mixer bowl and start mixing it with a paddle attachment, cooling it down to 55–60 °C / 131–140 °F.

8. When the choux paste has reached the required temperature, gradually, in small lots, start to add in the eggs, continuing to mix the choux paste at low speed.

   TIP
   - *The texture of the finished choux paste is checked visually, that's why you might need a little less egg mixture than is mentioned in the recipe. The choux paste should be smooth, homogeneous, glossy, and fall off the paddle as a ribbon, forming a sharp triangle. You may also notice some grains of rice flour in it. If you have used all the eggs and the right texture is still not achieved, you can add some warm milk, but such cases are extremely rare to happen.*

9. Pipe the finished gluten–free choux paste onto the baking mat according to the 'Piping the éclairs' section on page 11.

10. Bake the éclairs according to the instructions on page 12.

| MATCHA GLAZE

Ingredients	Total weight: ~ 655 g	100%
• Gelatin mass	70 g	10%
• Whipping cream 35%	90 g	14%
• Water	40 g	6%
• Glucose syrup	65 g	10%
• White chocolate Cacao Barry Zephyr 34%	200 g	31%
• Neutral glaze (nappage)	180 g	28%
• Matcha powder	10 g	1%

1. In a saucepan, combine cream, water and glucose syrup.

2. Heat the mixture over low heat to 80 °C / 176 °F and remove from the stove.

3. Add the gelatin mass and stir with a spatula until it has dissolved completely.

4. Combine the white chocolate and the neutral glaze in a measuring cup. Add in the matcha powder. Strain the hot cream mixture over the chocolate and neutral glaze.

5. Process everything with a hand blender at low speed, trying not to incorporate air bubbles, for 2–3 minutes until smooth.

6. Pour the finished glaze into a clean bowl, cover it with cling film touching the surface and put it in the fridge for at least 6 hours.

| MATCHA CUSTARD

Ingredients	Total weight: ~ 402 g	100%
• Milk 3.2%	250 g	62%
• Egg yolks	36 g	9%
• Sugar	21 g	5%
• Corn starch	18 g	4%
• Butter 82%	65 g	17%
• Gelatin mass	7 g	2%
• Matcha powder	5 g	1%

1. In a saucepan, heat the milk with matcha powder to 80 °C / 176 °F, take it off the heat.

2. In a separate bowl, combine sugar and cornstarch, add the egg yolks. Stir until a light mass is obtained.

3. Gradually strain the hot milk over the mixture of yolks, sugar and starch.

4. Pour the milk mixture back into the saucepan and cook the custard over low heat, constantly stirring, until it boils. After that, cook it for 1–2 minutes more.

5. Add the gelatin mass and stir until it has dissolved. Cool the custard down to 40 °C / 104 °F over a cold water bath, or leave it at room temperature, stirring occasionally to avoid skin forming.

6. Once the custard has cooled down, gradually add in the room temperature butter (18–20 °C / 64–68 °F) and stir with a whisk.

7. Transfer the finished custard to a clean and wide container and cool it down quickly. Cover it with cling film touching the surface and put it in the fridge or freezer for 10–15 minutes.

8. After cooling, the custard is ready to be used. If needed, it can be stored in the fridge for 48 hours.

| MATCHA SPONGE CAKE

Ingredients for 1 frame 20x20 cm	Total weight: ~ 402 g	100%
• Whole eggs	150 g	39%
• Sugar	75 g	19%
• Baking powder	1.5 g	<1%
• Almond powder	50 g	13%
• Rice flour	50 g	13%
• Grapeseed oil	50 g	13%
• Sea salt	1 g	<1%
• Matcha tea	6 g	2%
• Lemon zest	1 g	<1%

1. Put the eggs, sugar and salt in a bowl of a stand mixer. Beat the ingredients with a whisk attachment at maximum speed until a pale and fluffy foam is formed.

2. Heat the grapeseed oil to 40 °C / 104 °F, combine with lemon zest and add to the whipped egg mixture, mix until smooth.

3. In a bowl, mix sifted rice flour, almond powder, baking powder and matcha. Add the dry ingredients to the egg mixture and mix everything with a whisk.

4. Pour the sponge batter in a frame measuring 20x20 cm and spread it evenly using an offset spatula.

5. Bake the sponge in the oven, preheated to 160 °C / 320 °F, for 15–17 minutes. When ready, a skewer, inserted in the center of the sponge, should come out clean and dry.

6. Cool the sponge down at room temperature, then cut it into 20 strips 8x1 cm.

7. Place the leftover sponge in a food–processor and grind it into fine crumbs. Sift through a large sieve.

8. Dry the crumbs in the oven at 100 °C / 212 °F for about 1 hour.

| ASSEMBLING THE ÉCLAIRS

Ingredients

- Baked éclairs
- Baked matcha sponge strips
- Stabilized matcha custard

1. When the éclairs have cooled down, prepare them for filling. To do this, cut a strip 8 cm long and 1 cm wide from the bottom of each éclair. Keep the removed pieces of baked choux paste.

2. Transfer the matcha custard in the mixer bowl and mix with a whisk attachment at medium speed until smooth. The same can be made manually with a hand whisk. Take a pastry bag fitted with a round tip d=7 mm and fill 2/3 of it with the custard.

3. Fill the éclair with the custard by guiding the tip from one end to the other, leaving some space for the matcha sponge.

4. Insert a strip of matcha sponge inside each éclair and press slightly. Use the removed pieces of baked choux paste to seal the bottom.

5. Put the éclairs in the fridge to stabilize for a couple of minutes.

| GLAZING AND DECORATING THE ÉCLAIRS

Ingredients

- Filled cooled éclairs
- Stabilized matcha glaze
- Matcha sponge crumbs
- Matcha powder   50 g
- Gold leaf   Sufficient quantity

1. Heat the glaze to 26 °C / 79 °F and process it with a hand blender until smooth.

2. Dip each cooled éclair by 1/3 into the glaze. Carefully remove excess glaze by running your finger over the surface of the éclair.

3. Sprinkle the glaze with sponge crumbs and dust with matcha powder.

4. Place the gold leaf in the center of each éclair.

TIRAMISU ÉCLAIRS
for 15–20 éclairs 13 cm long

| CLASSIC ÉCLAIR CHOUX PASTE

1. To make the classic choux paste, follow the recipe on page 9.

2. Then pipe the éclairs according to the 'Piping the éclairs' section on page 11.

3. Finally, bake them according to the instructions on page 12.

| COFFEE–FLAVORED CUSTAR

Ingredients	Total weight: ~ 749 g	100%
• Sugar (1)	70 g	9%
• Milk 3.2%	180 g	24%
• Espresso	237 g	32%
• Cornstarch	33 g	4%
• Egg yolks	63 g	8%
• Sugar (2)	21 g	3%
• Sea salt	1 g	<1%
• Butter 82%	144 g	19%
• Vanilla	1 pod	<1%
• Milk 3.2% to compensate for the loss of liquid	Sufficient quantity	

1. In a saucepan, warm up the milk and espresso by almost bringing them to a boil. Remove the saucepan from the heat and set the mixture aside.

2. In a bowl, combine the cornstarch, sugar (2) and egg yolks, stir them with a whisk, but do not whip.

3. Pour sugar (1) into a separate saucepan. For a richer, more intense flavor, add vanilla seeds and the pod itself. Caramelize the sugar over medium heat, shaking the saucepan occasionally.

| COFFEE–FLAVORED CUSTARD

4. When the caramel acquires a nice amber color and starts to foam, pour the hot milk with espresso in it. Do this gradually, in several lots, stirring well with a whisk after each addition. Remove the mixture from the heat and strain it.

5. Weigh this mixture. In the process of caramelization some moisture evaporates, so it's necessary to add some milk to restore the initial weight of the mixture.

6. Gradually pour the hot mixture of milk, caramel and espresso into the mixture of yolks, sugar and starch.

7. Pour the mixture back in the saucepan, add salt. Bring the custard to a boil and cook it for 1.5–2 minutes over medium heat, constantly stirring with a whisk.

8. At first, the custard will thicken, and then, as it cooks, it will become more liquid. This is a sign that the starch has completely swollen. When this happens, remove the saucepan from the heat and cool the custard down to 40 °C / 104 °F over a cold water bath or at room temperature, stirring occasionally to prevent skin forming.

9. Add the room temperature butter (18–20 °C / 64–68 °F) in several portions, stirring well with a whisk.

10. Transfer the finished custard to a clean, wide container, and cover it with cling film touching the surface. Put it in the freezer or fridge for 15–20 minutes until it cools down completely.

| MASCARPONE CREAM

Ingredients	Total weight: ~ 336 g	100%
• Egg yolks	20 g	6%
• Sugar	11 g	3%
• Whipping cream 35%	55 g	16%
• Mascarpone cheese	250 g	74%

1. Mix sugar, egg yolks and whipping cream in a saucepan using a whisk. Start to heat the mixture over medium heat until it reaches 82 °C / 180 °F.

2. Pour the hot mixture over the mascarpone cheese and process with a hand blender until smooth.

3. Transfer the cream to a clean bowl, cover it with cling film and place it in the fridge for 6 hours to stabilize.

| LADYFINGER SPONGE

Ingredients	Total weight: ~ 418 g	100%
• Egg yolks	84 g	20%
• Sugar (1)	29 g	7%
• Egg whites	126 g	30%
• Egg white powder	4 g	<1%
• Sugar (2)	71 g	17%
• Flour T45	52 g	13%
• Potato starch	52 g	13%

1. Combine the sifted flour and starch using a whisk.

2. Place sugar (1) and egg yolks into the bowl of a stand mixer and whip with a whisk attachment until light and airy.

3. Meanwhile, whip the egg whites with sugar (2) and egg white powder into stiff peaks.

4. Gently combine the whipped egg yolks and egg whites using a silicone spatula.

5. Finally, add dry ingredients and mix with a spatula until smooth.

6. Pour the sponge batter on a silicone mat measuring 30x30 cm with borders h= 1 cm.

7. Bake the sponge in the oven, preheated to 170 °C / 338 °F, for 10–15 minutes.

8. Allow the baked sponge to cool down at room temperature, then cut it into strips measuring 10x1 cm.

| COFFEE SYRUP

Ingredients	Total weight: ~ 205 g	100%
• Espresso	150 g	73%
• Sugar	30 g	15%
• Coffee liqueur Amaretto	25 g	12%

1. Mix hot, freshly brewed espresso with sugar and stir until it has dissolved.

2. Cool the coffee with sugar to 40 °C / 104 °F and add the liqueur.

3. Use the syrup at room temperature (18–20 °C / 64–68 °F).

4. If desired, you can store the finished syrup in a closed container at 3 °C / 37 °F for no longer than 72 hours.

Tiramisu Éclairs
for 15–20 éclairs 13 cm long

| ASSEMBLING AND DECORATING THE ÉCLAIRS

Ingredients

- Baked éclairs
- Chilled coffee–flavored custard
- Baked ladyfinger sponge strips
- Coffee syrup
- Stabilized mascarpone cream
- Cocoa powder   50 g

1. When the éclairs have cooled down, prepare them for filling. To do this, cut a strip 8 cm long and 1 cm wide from the top of each éclair.

2. Stir the custard with a whisk until smooth and transfer it to a pastry bag fitted with a round tip d=7 mm.

3. Fill 2/3 of the éclairs with the custard.

4. Soak the sponge strips with coffee syrup and dip them into the custard. Using an offset spatula, smooth the top of the éclairs and remove excess cream, if any.

5. Transfer the mascarpone cream into the bowl of a stand mixer and whip it with a whisk attachment until light and airy.

6. Fill the piping bag, fitted with a Closed Star tip d=12 mm, with mascarpone cream and pipe it on top of the éclairs.

7. Dust the éclairs with some cocoa powder.

VANILLA ÉCLAIRS

for 15–20 éclairs 13 cm long

| GELATIN MASS

Ingredients	Total weight: ~ 14 g	100%
• Powdered gelatin 200 Bloom	2 g	14%
• Cold water	12 g	86%

1. Pour the powdered gelatin into a clean container and add cold water. Gently stir with a whisk.

2. Place the mixture in the fridge for 10–15 minutes to allow the gelatin to swell and bloom.

3. Take the mass out of the fridge and melt it in the microwave. If there is any foam, remove it with a sieve. Then place the mass back in the fridge to let it set completely.

4. Use scissors to cut the gelatin mass into cubes — this way, you can weigh it and it's more convenient to work with. The ratio of gelatin to water should always be 1:6 (one part gelatin to six parts water).

5. You can make the gelatin mass in advance and store it in the fridge for up to 2 days.

TIP
• *If you're using gelatin leaves instead, take the same weight as you would with powdered gelatin and soak the leaves in cold water. The gelatin leaves should absorb exactly the right amount of water they need. Then squeeze them and use as required.*

| CLASSIC ÉCLAIR CHOUX PASTE

1. To make the classic choux paste, follow the recipe on page 9.

2. Then pipe the éclairs according to the 'Piping the éclairs' section on page 11.

3. Finally, bake them according to the instructions on page 12.

| VANILLA CUSTARD

Ingredients	Total weight: ~ 888 g	100%
• Milk 3.2%	400 g	45%
• Whipping cream 35%	100 g	11%
• Egg yolks	80 g	9%
• Sugar	94 g	10%
• Cornstarch	40 g	5%
• Butter 82%	110 g	12%
• Gelatin mass	14 g	2%
• Greek yogurt	50 g	6%
• Vanilla	2 pods	<1%

1. In a saucepan, heat the milk and cream, as well as vanilla seeds and the pods, to 80 °C / 176 °F. Remove the saucepan from the heat, cover it with cling film and let the mixture infuse for 30 minutes.

2. In a separate bowl, combine sugar and cornstarch, add the egg yolks. Stir until a light mass is obtained.

3. Reheat the vanilla–flavored milk and cream to 80 °C / 176 °F. Then gradually strain the hot mixture over the mixture of yolks, sugar and starch.

4. Pour the milk and cream mixture back into the saucepan and cook the custard over low heat, constantly stirring, until it boils. After that, cook it for 1–2 minutes more.

| VANILLA CUSTARD

5. Add the gelatin mass and stir until it has dissolved. Cool the custard down to 40 °C / 104 °F over a cold water bath, or leave it at room temperature, stirring occasionally to avoid skin forming.

6. Once the custard has cooled down, gradually add the room temperature butter (18–20 °C / 64–68 °F) and stir with a whisk.

7. Add greek yogurt and stir with a whisk once again.

8. Transfer the finished custard to a clean and wide container and cool it down quickly. Cover it with cling film touching the surface and put it in the fridge or freezer for 10–15 minutes.

9. After cooling, the custard is ready to be used. If needed, it can be stored in the fridge for 48 hours.

| ASSEMBLING THE ÉCLAIRS

Ingredients

• Baked éclairs
• Chilled vanilla custard

1. When the éclairs have cooled down, prepare them for filling. To do this, use a needle tip and make three holes in the bottom part of the éclair: two of them close to the edges and one in the middle. These three holes will help you to fill each éclair fully.

2. Transfer the custard to a mixer bowl and stir it with a whisk attachment at high speed or by hand until smooth. Fill a pastry bag fitted with a round tip d=7 mm with the finished custard 2/3 full.

3. Fill each hole of the éclair with the custard until you feel it is full.

| ASSEMBLING THE ÉCLAIRS

4. Clean off the bottom of the éclairs with an offset spatula, transfer the éclairs to a baking sheet and put them in the fridge for 5–10 minutes until the custard stabilizes.

| WHITE ICING

Ingredients	Total weight: ~ 280 g	100%
Sugar	200 g	72%
Water	40 g	14%
Glucose syrup	40 g	14%

1. Combine all ingredients in a saucepan and bring them to 117 °C / 243 °F.

2. Pour the syrup into a mixer bowl and let it cool down to 43 °C / 109 °F.

3. Using a paddle attachment, start mixing the syrup at low speed, gradually incrcasing the speed to medium. Whip until the syrup has crystallized completely. The finished icing should thicken and turn white.

4. Pour the icing into a clean container, close the lid and set it aside for 24 hours at room temperature.

❘ CHOCOLATE ICING

Ingredients	Total weight: ~ 155 g	100%
• Sugar	100 g	64%
• Water	20 g	13%
• Glucose syrup	20 g	13%
• Cocoa powder	15 g	10%

1. Combine all ingredients in a saucepan and bring them to 117 °C / 243 °F.

2. Pour the syrup into a mixer bowl and let it cool down to 43 °C / 109 °F.

3. Using a paddle attachment, start mixing the syrup at low speed, gradually increasing the speed to medium. Whip until the syrup has crystallized completely. The finished icing should thicken.

4. Pour the icing into a clean container, close the lid and set it aside for 24 hours at room temperature.

GLAZING THE ÉCLAIRS

Ingredients

- Chilled assembled éclairs
- White icing
- Chocolate icing

1. Warm the white icing to a temperature of 35 °C / 95 °F. Its texture should resemble condensed milk or honey.

2. Dip the cooled éclairs into the white icing by 1/3. Carefully remove excess coating by running your finger over the surface of the éclair.

3. Warm the chocolate icing to 35 °C / 95 °F, transfer it to a paper cornet and pipe thin lines across the éclair. Using a toothpick, make a spider web pattern.

Made in the USA
Monee, IL
09 May 2025

17175871R00069